The DiamondLight Princess

by Michael Patterson,
illustrated by Alicia Yaiza

© 2014, All Rights Reserved

Available at Amazon.com and other fine bookstores

© 2014, All Rights Reserved, Michael Patterson and Alicia Yaiza
ISBN-13: 9781494409579
A production of Cedargrove

Did you ever notice that nobody is like anybody else?

Everybody has their own special abilities, that nobody else has. Everybody has their own special gifts, which only they can give to other people. If they don't give those gifts, nobody else can, and people get sad, without those presents, because presents make our lives special.

This is a story about a princess with a very special gift.

4

The DiamondLight Princess

Once up on a time, long ago, and far away, there was a crystal castle. In that castle lived a very special princess. She had eyes, just like your eyes, or maybe, the eyes of your sister. Her hair was actually like your hair, or maybe, your sister's hair. She almost always had a very big smile.

The princess had a very special name: the DiamondLight Princess, because she had a very special ability. She seemed to be full of wonderful colors, just like a diamond, in sunlight.

The colors flowed out of her heart, all over her, and then over others. She seemed to have so many wonderful colors! Wherever she went, her footsteps were full of colors. Whatever she touched with her hands would be full of wonderful colors, too. Anything she looked at started getting new, wonderful colors. The more she looked, the brighter the colors were.

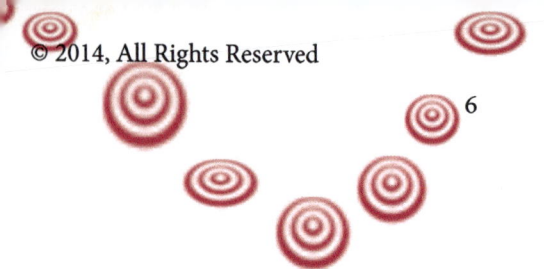

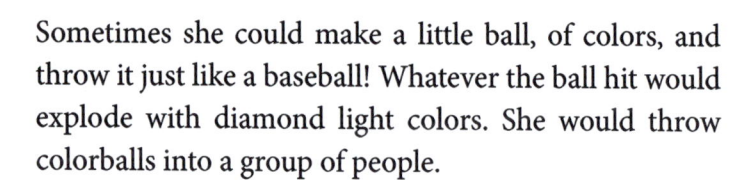

Sometimes she could make a little ball, of colors, and throw it just like a baseball! Whatever the ball hit would explode with diamond light colors. She would throw colorballs into a group of people.

They would smile, their clothes would look bright and new, and their faces would fill up with light. They would be so much kinder to each other, and help each other more, for a while.

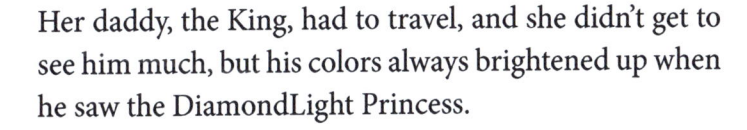

Her daddy, the King, had to travel, and she didn't get to see him much, but his colors always brightened up when he saw the DiamondLight Princess.

She would look at flowers in the royal garden, and smile at them, and the flowers would get even more beautiful, because they wanted to. When the DiamondLight Princess smiled, the flowers wanted to be more beautiful than the best they could imagine.

People would see her throw a colorball into the sky, at dawn, or sunset, and the Sun would make the most incredibly beautiful colors in the sky.

Everybody loved the DiamondLight Princess, so much, because she filled up their lives with so much light, and love.

Everybody would say "Hi Princess Di! [which is short for DiamondLight] to her, when they saw her. She reminded them how the light they had in themselves felt.

Many people thought she was putting the beautiful colors into other things. She wasn't, though. She knew a special secret. She knew that everything has wonderful colors, already, just under the surface. The colors are waiting for someone to notice them.

When she saw the beautiful colors, in a relaxed, playful way, they leaped out, so everybody could see them! The colorballs she threw were only a way to get other people to pay attention to the colors in something, so the colors could leap out. She tried to explain this, but people didn't understand. They loved the beautiful colors, though.

One person, the gardener, was very jealous of the DiamondLight Princess. He couldn't make the colors come out in flowers, the way Princess Di could.

The DiamondLight Princess tried to explain that the colors were already there. She would say, "All you have to do is see the colors, when you feel relaxed, and happy in your heart, and they come out". The gardener was angry. He was convinced that the DiamondLight Princess had a special secret magic powder, to make the colors come. He was convinced that she was lying to him, even though she wasn't. The gardener was angry.

The gardener started studying sorcery, so he could make the magic powder, but he couldn't figure out how. One day, the DiamondLight Princess was walking in the garden, by herself. The gardener grabbed her, and demanded that she give him the magic powder. The princess tried to smile at him, to wake up the colors in him. He was so angry and so tense, that it didn't work. He threw her down, on the ground, and yelled at her, and the DiamondLight Princess was really scared. Nobody had ever hurt her before.

12

The royal guards came and took the gardener away. But the DiamondLight Princess was so scared, she couldn't see the light in people any more. She felt very sad, and mad. She thought she was bad.

The Queen tried to explain to the DiamondLight Princess that she wasn't bad, that it wasn't her fault. But Princess Di thought she was bad. She was so busy feeling bad, she forgot to play with colors and light. She couldn't go to the garden any more, she felt so bad. Dark colors gathered where she had been thrown down.

Even the King had dark colors, sometimes. Sometimes her mom, the Queen, looked like she had been crying.

Other people told her it wasn't her fault, that the gardener had filled his heart with resentment, and hatred, but she still felt that somehow she was bad. The King and Queen were sad, and mad, and sad, and mad.

The people in the village outside the castle were sad, and mad, and sad, because they didn't get to see the diamond light. For a long time, everybody was mad, and sad, and sad, and mad. They would argue. Sometimes they would go to a special room at the court, to argue about the gardener.

Some people would say that the gardener didn't have a dad, he just grew up with his mom, and that made him mad, so he did bad things. Other people said the gardener should be branded, so everybody would know how bad he was. The gardener said that if he couldn't have the magic powder, that made the DiamondLight colors, then nobody could.

16

One day, a traveler from somewhere else came to the castle. He said he had seen another crystal castle in another kingdom, with beautiful diamond light colors around it. He said that they had magicians there, who could help the DiamondLight Princess get her special diamond light colors back.

The DiamondLight Princess said, "I don't deserve the light. I was punished, so I must have been bad, and bad people don't deserve the light". The Queen and King immediately told Princess Di she was good, but the princess wouldn't listen.

Princess Di said she didn't want to deal with magic people, because the gardener was a sorcerer. The Queen said the princess didn't have to ever deal with magic people again, if she didn't want to.

So the people were mad, and sad, and sad, and mad. The DiamondLight Princess was mostly sad. She tried to live normally, but it wasn't easy. She kept thinking about the gardener. Sometimes Princess Di would hear the Queen, her mom, and the King, her dad, saying really angry things.

They had to go to a special room in the court, sometimes, where a bailiff would ask the gardener questions, and the gardener would talk to a Court Liar. Sometimes the Court Liar would even blame the DiamondLight Princess, for not giving the magic powder to the gardener. The DiamondLight Princess would explain there was no such powder.

Sometimes it seemed like the Court Liar was as bad as the gardener. The Queen told Princess Di to just answer the Liar's questions.

The DiamondLight Princess was tired of everything. She missed her beautiful colors, and her heart felt empty without them. So one day, she told her mom, the Queen, that she could go to the castle with her, to talk to one of the magicians. She thought it would be nice to get her colors back.

The Queen agreed to get the royal coach, to go to the other crystal castle. She said the DiamondLight Princess would have to be very brave, because sometimes the magicians would have to talk to the princess without her mother being in the room. So the Queen packed up a lunch, and off they went.

The coach went over the dirt roads, by meadows, through forests, and finally it came to a beautiful crystal castle, surrounded by diamond light colors, though they weren't as bright as the DiamondLight Princess remembered. She got to thinking that maybe one of the magicians could help her.

She went with her mother, the Queen, to the stairs that led to the door. They were big stairs. The stairs were so tall, and the princess was small, afraid she'd fall. She thought she was just a small princess, and couldn't climb it.

Then she thought, well, but we came all this way, let's keep going. She had a little snack from her lunch, and drank some water.

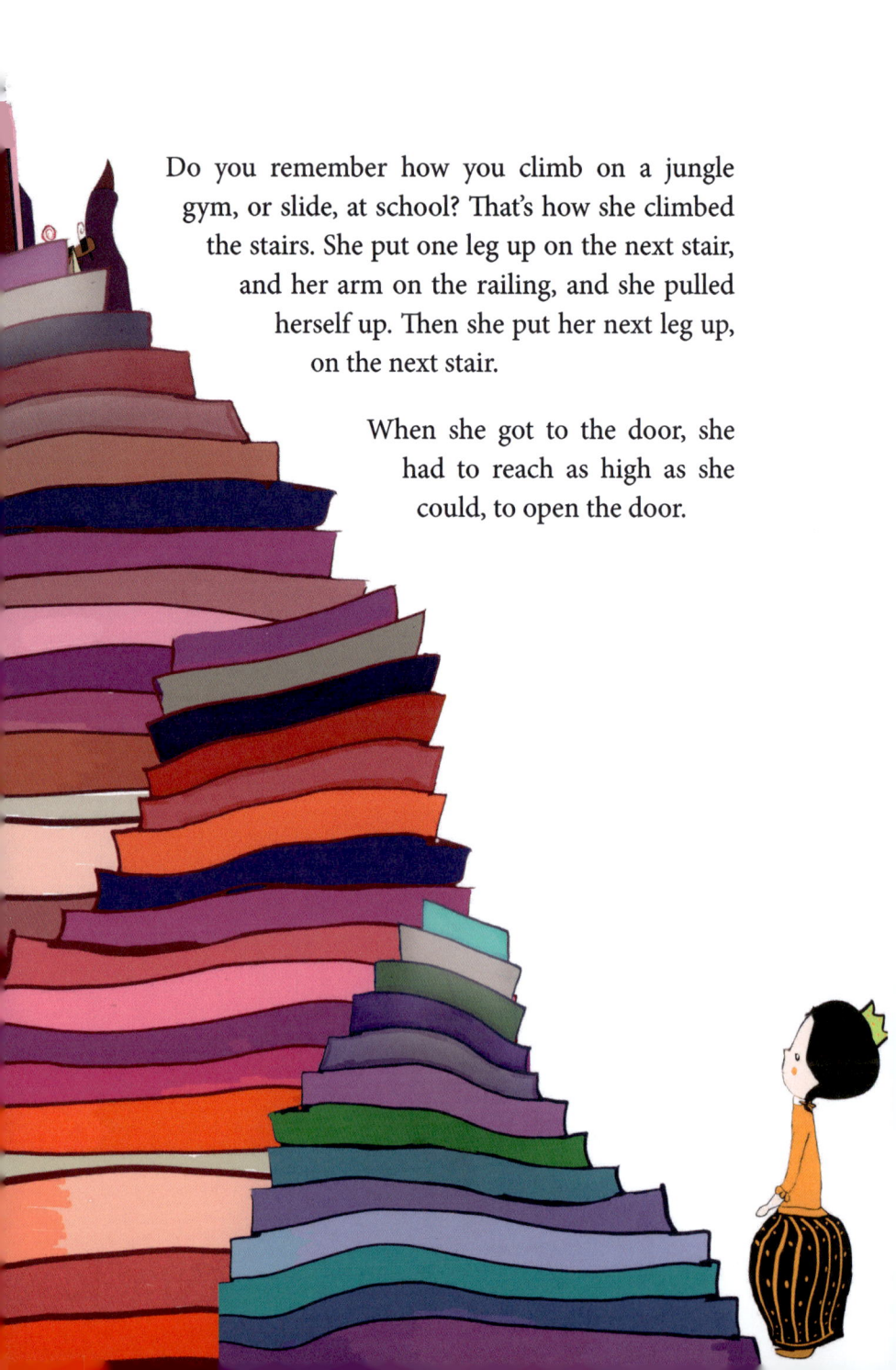

Do you remember how you climb on a jungle gym, or slide, at school? That's how she climbed the stairs. She put one leg up on the next stair, and her arm on the railing, and she pulled herself up. Then she put her next leg up, on the next stair.

When she got to the door, she had to reach as high as she could, to open the door.

She opened the door, and there were even more stairs to climb. She climbed them in the same way, climbing and climbing, till she felt like she could touch the clouds.

She finally got to the room of the magician. She went in, and there were more guards.

One guard asked her mother, the Queen, for the special royal pass, that would allow the princess to see the magician. Then they asked the Queen to fill out some magic papers, to help the magician see how to do the magic.

The DiamondLight Princess then heard the door open. She felt a light feeling in her stomach, that some call butterflies. She was a little bit worried- was the magician a good magician, or a bad magician? Her mom, the Queen, thought it would be ok. The princess wasn't sure.

24

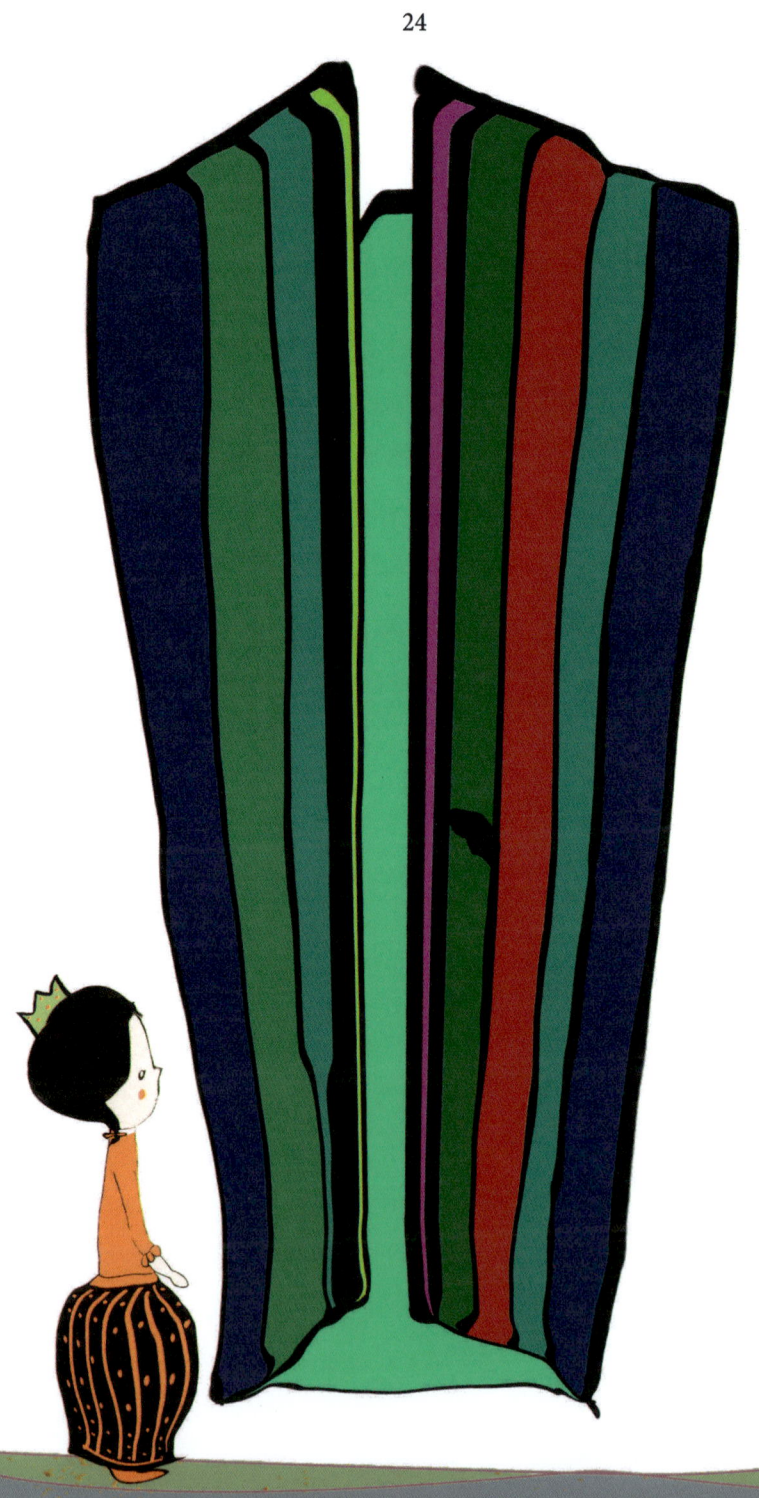

A guard took them to see the magician. She went into the magician's room, which was made of stone, and had a desk. The DiamondLight Princess looked at the magician. She thought the magician was good. She used a special trick that another princess had told her. You know, when you tell the truth, from your heart, there is a special light in your eyes, and face, and you feel light. When you tell a lie, especially a lie that hurts people, the light goes off, and your face looks murky and shady, and you feel heavy. She thought the magician was good, because she saw the light, like that, and she felt light.

The magician smiled at the DiamondLight Princess, and said, "I'm so glad you could come here. Would you like to sit in the big magic chair, the one that pulls out all the heavy feelings, and the feelings that feel bad?"

The DiamondLight Princess said she would, so she did. Her feet didn't even touch the floor, as she sat in the chair.

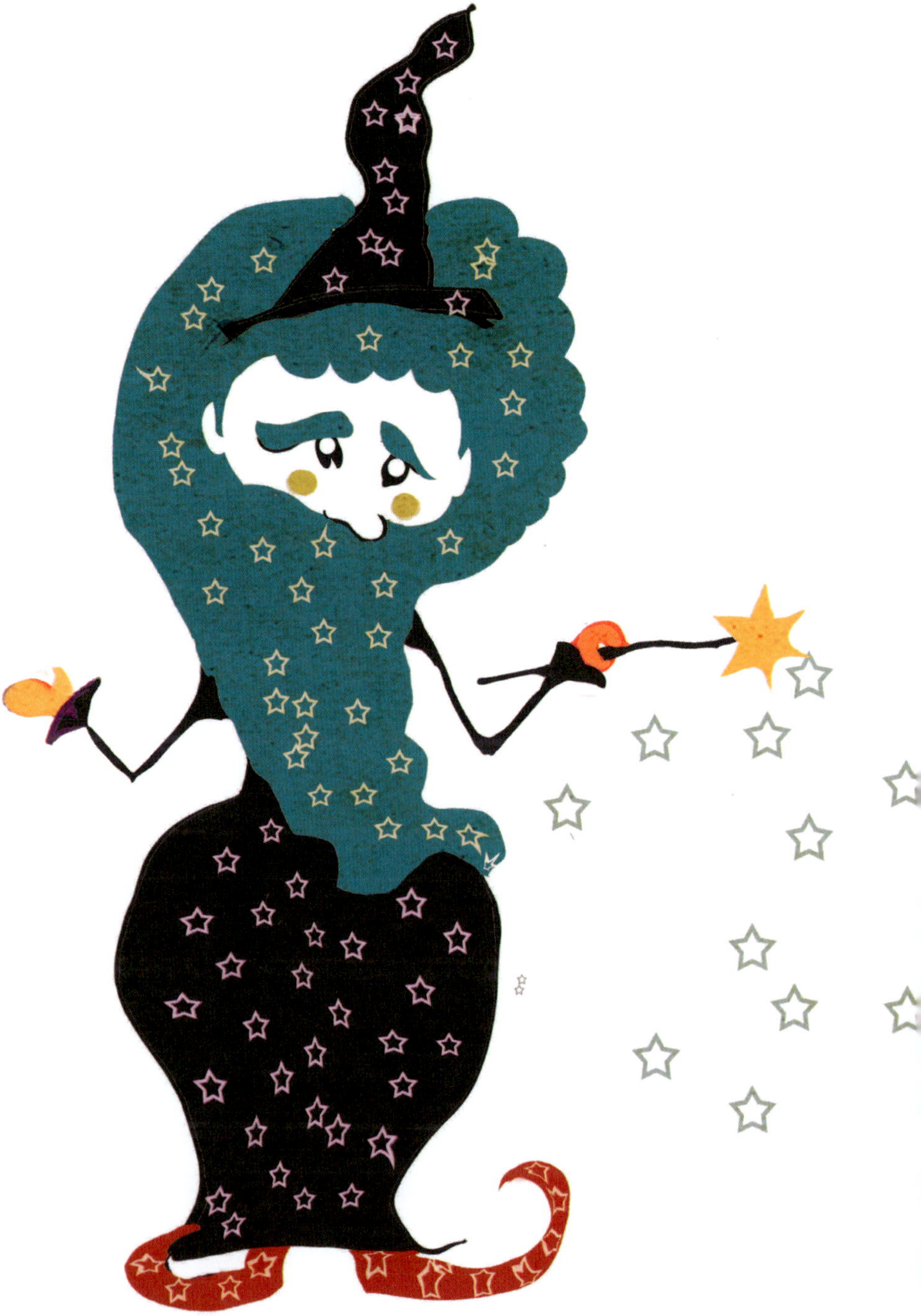

The magician said, "I wonder, could it be that you came all this way, to get your magic colors back?". The DiamondLight Princess said, "Yes, I would like them back, they felt so good".

The magician said, "I will tell you the Secret about how to get your colors back. I have to tell you a few other secrets, first, though. Is that ok?" The DiamondLight Princess said it was ok.

So the magician told her secrets, and many secrets, all about her. The DiamondLight Princess thought they were interesting.

Then the magician said, "And I know the real secret you want, is how to get the DiamondLight colors back, isn't that right?" Princess Di said, "Yes".

So the magician said, "Remember when you look at a flower, in bright sunlight, how it glows?" Princess Di said, "Yes, I liked that". The magician said, "OK, put your hands on your heart, and feel the love you used to feel, for the plants, and people, and your family, and animals".

Princess Di did this. For a moment, she thought she saw the DiamondLight colors.

The magician said, "Did you see the DiamondLight colors, even if only for one second?" Princess Di said, "Yes".

The magician said, "Can you breathe deeply, and without trying hard, feel those feelings again flowing in your heart?" Princess Di did this. All of a sudden, the DiamondLight colors showed up, but then they faded.

The magician smiled, and said, "The gardener thought you had magic powder. But you know that you didn't have magic powder. You just let the DiamondLight colors flow in your heart, and when you sprayed the colors on other things, the colors in those other things woke up, so everybody could see them.

You have a very special gift, to give to the world. Your gift is to help people see that they have the DiamondLight colors in them, too. When you wake up the colors, in things, other people know it is possible. Some people believe they can do it, and they start practicing.

Wouldn't it be fun to play with other kids, to make DiamondLight colors appear? Because when many people do it, it's a lot more fun, and many, many more colors show up! In fact, if you get enough people together, you can throw enough colors at the gardener, so even the gardener can play with DiamondLight!"

The magician said, "You and other people thought your colors went away. But they didn't go away. It was like the love and light in your heart turned off, after you were hurt, and they didn't come out any more.

The magic colors are still there. All you have to do is turn on your heart faucet, and they come out again, just like before! Would you like to know how to turn the faucet of the colors on, in your heart?" Princess Di said, "Oh yes!"

The magician said, "Just put your hands on your heart. Breathe deeply".

The DiamondLight Princess

31

32

"Relax. Know that the colors are there, they were always there, they are still there, and they will always be there. Do you remember that special feeling, in your heart, when you were flowing colors everywhere? You can do this now. The colors are still hiding in everything. Just feel the flow, and the colors wake up, just like they did before! Take some time- just feel the flow. There's no trying, you just relax, and the flow comes, naturally. That's how you open up your heart faucet".

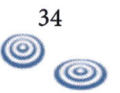

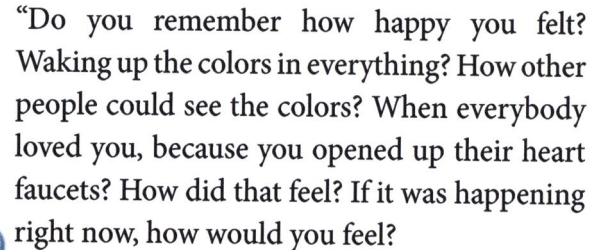

"Do you remember how happy you felt? Waking up the colors in everything? How other people could see the colors? When everybody loved you, because you opened up their heart faucets? How did that feel? If it was happening right now, how would you feel?

If your mommy, the Queen, and daddy, the King, and everybody else knew you had your colors back, think how happy they would feel!"

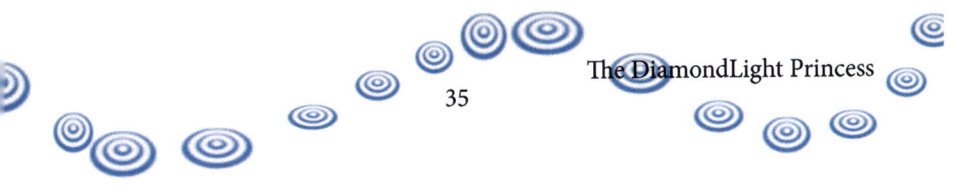

The DiamondLight Princess relaxed, and breathed deeply, and felt the flow. All of a sudden, she realized her colors were back! She could flow colors to everything around her!

The magician said, "I think what the gardener did was very bad. I don't know what the court will do. What is really important, here, is to realize you are here, now, and you can choose to open your heart faucet, and be happier than you were before.

Now you know that maybe a few people have stuck heart faucets, and get jealous, because they think they can't play with colors".

36

"What you can do is to work with other people, who know how to play with colors, and pour colours into the people who think they can't play with colors. Fill them with so many colors they can't keep it bottled up inside, any more. Maybe we can have a kingdom where everybody has their heart faucet on, I don't know".

The DiamondLight Princess could feel the colors coming out of her heart, almost like a firehose.

She made a colorball, and threw it at the window- and it brightened up! She flowed colors into her clothing, and it looked bright and radiant!

She threw a big colorball, and it went up to the sky, and made a rainbow! It worked!

The DiamondLight Princess said, "Thank you! Thank you for giving my colors back to me!"

And the magician said, "I didn't give them back to you. I only showed you that you had them all the time! They were in you all the time, and are always with you! All you have to do is turn the faucet on, in your heart!"

The magician said, "Maybe you want to show your mommy, the Queen, that you are playing with your colors again. I bet she'd be really happy! And maybe one day, you might come back and visit, because, you know, you are very, very good with colors, and I'd like to learn about colors from you! Magicians always want to learn more".

Princess Di said she would. She kind of liked the magician, who was goofy, in a funny way.

So she left the magician's room, and closed the door gently, like a good princess.

Princess Di felt taller, somehow, and the stairs felt smaller, and it was so easy to go down the stairs. She looked up at her mom, the Queen, and filled her mom with colors, and her mom looked so happy, she cried! I don't know how that happened.

So she went home, with her Mom, in the royal coach, by the forests, by the meadows, over the dirt roads, till she came back to the royal crystal castle.

She flowed her colors at the castle, and realized they flowed like a firehose, better than ever before! The castle glowed, with color!

The people in the village saw the DiamondLight Princess, and said, "Oh, she's back!"

She looked at them, and saw the light in them, and they exploded in beautiful colors, and the people said, "Oh, she has her colors back, too! Yippeeeeeeee!" They were very glad, they weren't sad any more.

And when the King saw her, he was so happy she had her colors back, he smiled, and his own colors got bright! The DiamondLight Princess was happy to see that, and she hugged her dad, the King.

The DiamondLight Princess went to the place in the garden, where the gardener threw her down, and she let all the dark colors there vanish, and she filled them up with bright colors.

She filled up the entire crystal castle with newer, brighter colors. She asked the colors to get brighter, better than the best she could imagine, and they did!

The DiamondLight Princess saw the gardener again, later, in the court. But she wasn't afraid, because the magician had told her secrets.

The magician had told her that when you go to school, you learn what they teach, you learn your letters, and words, and how to read. Some people don't learn their lessons very well. The gardener was so angry when he was young, he didn't hear his lessons. One lesson is that you can't take other people's colors, it never works.

The magician said, "The gardener tried to take your colors, and only took his own colors out of his world. His world is grey because he closed his own heart faucet. He has to go to a special school, for a long time, to learn this.

The good students know that you open up your heart faucet, and then your own colors flow. When you have a good teacher, with her heart faucet on, you remember to turn your own heart faucet on!"

The DiamondLight Princess wasn't afraid of the gardener any more, because she understood that the gardener didn't listen to his lessons, or maybe didn't understand the lessons, and didn't remember to ask questions about what he didn't understand.

44

Things weren't quite the same any more, in the kingdom, but it didn't matter, because the DiamondLight Princess knew she could make the world a better place, with her special gifts. She could actually make the world better than it was, by helping people wake up the colors in their own lives!

The DiamondLight Princess studied colors, and got better and better. She decided to teach as many people as she could, about opening up their heart faucets, and spraying colors everywhere.

She finally opened her own school to teach people how to play with DiamondLight, to open up their heart faucets. The students got very good at it. The people in the kingdom were very happy, and the kingdom was a very happy place to live.

The children who learned how to play with light got better and better at it.

46

And that is the end of the story. Or is it? This storyteller can tell this story, because he met the DiamondLight Princess. She showed him how to open up his heart faucet, and to wake up the colors in other people, and places.

How would you feel, if you could flow the DiamondLight colors through your own heart faucet, right now? Because you can, if you want to. Sometimes just being kind opens up people's heart faucets. Sometimes if you just ask, "How does it get better than this?", things get better.

When I was in college, my parents' home was certified as a foster home by the state. The state often needed to place teenage girls who had been in bad situations. Usually, it was a case of a divorced mother, with children, who had a boyfriend, a "gardener", who treated the child badly. I see gardeners, and diamondlight princesses, even where I live, now. It is sad. People are sad, and mad, and mad, and sad, and their colors are grey. But I remember what the DiamondLight Princess that I met told me. So, I turned on my heart faucet, to get ideas. That is how I put this together.

Experience is experience. Trauma is trauma. What stays with us is the judgment, the meaning we assign to it. The same trauma is interpreted by one person as destroying their life permanently. By another person, it is just another event, for to them, the best steel takes the hottest fire and the hardest blows.

I have studied several "magician" modalities, and reframing experience can make trauma much easier to deal with, no matter how painful. The Japanese filmmaker Akira Kurosawa had a consistent message, in his movies. That message was that outside is only chaos. The only place we can ever find order, beauty, discipline, and everything else that makes life worthwhile, is inside. This story is designed to give some order, to the chaos. Perhaps it's just bullying, or shaming, or belittling people. Perhaps it is worse. I don't understand why some people treat each other so badly. It is so much more fun to be kind.

So we deal with that. There is a happy ending- you find deep inner resources, and pull them out. This does not excuse what the gardeners do. However, the princesses need to adjust, if they are going to live their lives. I can't solve everyone's problems, and maybe I can't solve anybody's problems. However, I can wake up colors, in people… just as I was taught by the first DiamondLight Princess I met, who was in her 20's when I first knew her, waking up the colors in a whole range of people. It took me about 25 years to match her abilities. My daughters are pretty good at playing with DiamondLight, also.

This story is an example of Ericksonian therapeutic storytelling. Generally, these stories are "healing stories". It may be better to vary some, from the text, according to the situation. Perhaps the best easy-to-read book on the healing techniques of Milton Erickson is the book *My Voice will go with you*, by Sidney Rosen, though there are many others. The books *Coyote Medicine*, by Lewis Mehl-Madrona, and *Therapeutic Metaphors*, by Gordon, discuss the use of therapeutic storytelling, as well.

Certain issues of psychological trauma, in what Carl Jung called the psychological shadow, can only be gotten at metaphorically, as Jung pointed out. This story is one example of the use of metaphor, as one way to ease the pain of severe psychological trauma. This is only a sample of metaphor, presented only as an example. Metaphor is best drawn from the particulars of a situation, and as with any magic- the magician would never explain the trick.

Imagination, to Sufis, is shaping the clay of potential. Perhaps, just perhaps, it's not just your imagination, perhaps it is something more… Metaphor does far more than we know. And how will you have fun playing with magic colors, yourself? Maybe this whole story is just a story about playing with color, and perspectives…What are the infinite possibilities? How much fun could a person have, playing with metaphor? and DiamondLight?

Michael Patterson

© 2014, All Rights Reserved

Printed in Great Britain
by Amazon